PAPER TRAILS

SUBASH M R

Copyright © Subash M R
All Rights Reserved.

This book has been published with all efforts taken to make the material error-free after the consent of the author. However, the author and the publisher do not assume and hereby disclaim any liability to any party for any loss, damage, or disruption caused by errors or omissions, whether such errors or omissions result from negligence, accident, or any other cause.

While every effort has been made to avoid any mistake or omission, this publication is being sold on the condition and understanding that neither the author nor the publishers or printers would be liable in any manner to any person by reason of any mistake or omission in this publication or for any action taken or omitted to be taken or advice rendered or accepted on the basis of this work. For any defect in printing or binding the publishers will be liable only to replace the defective copy by another copy of this work then available.

To dear wife and Abhi.

Contents

Foreword

The Blogospheres author strikes into again with Paper Trails, thereby causing a strong emotion in readers mind.

Paper Trails occur suddenly with no time from release of the Blogospheres, the first book of this very same author in this series, and have beneficial effects on readers' mind.

It is sure that readers may again be struck by Paper Trails as interesting and impressive. Paper Trails has presented quite a challenging and daunting experiences imprinted on the mind of author.

CHAPTER ONE

Aunt and Uncle

What a ridiculous behavior it is when a ten years boy or girl addresses a boy or girl of the same age as aunt or uncle, who are unknown to them, when they come across the latter in a family mall or a multiplex. Here, who should be blamed? Who else, except the child's parents (young)? In their social dictionary, there is no other form of address except aunt or uncle to a male or female person irrespective of their age.

Aunt and Uncle

It is the limitation of the English language, wherein we cannot see *anna*, *thamma*, *akka* and *thangi*! Aunt or uncle are not certainly disgraceful words, but some people use it inappropriately and thereby ridicule others. Children are innocent, but they are tutored by their mechanical parents as to how to address an unfamiliar person. If the person is a male irrespective of his age addresses him as uncle or if the person is a female irrespective of her age addresses her as aunt. This is definitely not our culture hundred percent. It may have been imported. But, very embarrassing indeed.

Warning

We are transforming into a Sir-Calling culture automatically, and we don't even mind calling a street beggar sir or madam without a second thought. But this so-called aunt or uncle always bothers others particularly riders of two-wheeler or drivers of four-wheeler!? To be precise, while riding a bike or driving a car towards one's destination, who will be prepared to give coins to those said aunt or uncle? Is it practical to give away something to them who come to you at no time clear traffic signal or in a slow-moving traffic road! If I am personally inclined to give changes to them on route to my office, it is not possible either because of about to clear traffic signal or practical inconvenience? In either case, result will be disappointment and mood out, thinking of not giving pittance to those unclassified people who will not be seen only in airway traffic.

Unlike dowry, begging is not a sin; but definitely a crime under the law, like dowry. Both, giving and accepting dowry is punishable, similarly, not only begging but also giving to the beggar is a crime. I have personally no problem to provide some money which is in excess with me to someone with dare exigencies. In that sense, donation is not begging. Therefore, it is not a sin like dowry.

Political funding and political debating are new trends which we are going through now?! In any case, common man is always in a dilemma. No day is exempted from such hour long debating and it will go on and on as first, second and third, etc. Spin-doctoring and impartiality will not go hand in hand. Spin doctors who leave no stone upturned. They will speak anything under the sun. Without them, TV Channels are like nests without birds.

In the name of breaking news, anything can be published or aired should not be the motto of a journalist. Look at the nature. She is the best news setter we have ever seen till date in terms of setting up of everything in order in her canvas. Take a small example. Animals are placed in jungle. Fishes are kept apart in water. Men are dumped in surface. If anybody will supersede this order of nature in one another for breaking news in the name of sensational journalism, what would be the outcome? Piss-up. The synonymy between a magnet and a journalist is that the former attracts iron and the latter goes behind the breaking news.

Judiciary is becoming newsy field nowadays. Where cost and adjournment are always bone of contentious matters. Recently a famous high court judge has passed orders imposing of cost to himself against the seven-judge bench of the Supreme Court that is hearing the case against him. Even stranger than this is that wherein another famous high court judge has adjourned a pending case to more than three and a half years?!These are the occasions wherein rule of law is challenged. The thought process of judge is above the law is unhealthy not only to the judiciary but also to the society. Judicial decisions pronounced on the spur of the moment is not always good in law.

Robert Gascoyne-Cecil

The world is heading over heels, but our leaders are still living king-size in good old days! In democracy, victory of a proposed representative depends upon votes (majority) of his electorate. The electors are giving mandate to their MLAs or MPs not to slap them, but to serve and represent them. If they go against the cardinal prepositions of the democracy FOR, BY and OF, then, the voter with his four-letter digging arm 'VOTE' will scoop up the former from the power forever. When, no Uncle Sam will be there to rescue!

CHAPTER TWO

DELAYED JUSTICE AND HURRIED JUSTICE

Can delay in justice dispensation system be excused thinking the old age saying that better late than never? But, remember that justice delayed is justice denied. A person had to fight a legal (civil) battle for 40 years to regain possession of a shop he had rented out forty years ago. What a sorrow state of affairs does this delay causes to the poor litigants?

Snail

Delay in criminal trial violates the right guaranteed under Article.21 of Constitution of India. Protection of life and personal liberty. No person shall be deprived of his life or personal liberty except according to procedure established by law. But, in fact, one person or other is destined to litigate for more than three or four decades to get appropriate relief or reliefs in a case irrespective of civil or criminal from a competent court of law ranging from lower court to Supreme Court in India. It is definitely very unfortunate and sorrow state of affairs.

The Justice League

Each year, the World Justice Project surveys 99 countries to come up with their Rule of Law Index. The index is used by policy wonks and analysts to dig deeper into why some countries are better at protecting civil liberties than others, and where countries rank in comparison to similar income countries nearby. The U.S. ranks high among the 99, but discrimination in the criminal justice system keeps it out of the top 10. Here's the world's justice league, and a look at some of the stragglers.

No. 10: Singapore

Singapore has a global ranking of 10. It scores best on matters of order and security, criminal justice, and corruption. For example, when asked if they felt safe or very safe when walking home at night, 94% said yes. Only 4% said they were the victim of an armed robbery in the last three years. On matters of political corruption, 73% of respondents said politicians would be prosecuted and punished, well above the average response of countries in Southeast Asia.

No. 9: Germany

Germany scores best overall on matters of civil justice and constraints of government power. On matters of corruption, more than half of Germans (59%) surveyed said political officials would be prosecuted and face jail time for crimes against the state, which is greater than the average in Western Europe. No one in Germany sees bribery within the courts as a problem either. What do Germans agree most upon about their country's legal protections? Labor unions. When asked if workers in Germany can freely form labor unions and bargain for their rights with their employers, 95% of them said they agreed.

No. 8: Australia

Australia ranks highest on matters related to the government, from its positively viewed regulatory environment, to checks and balances within the government apparatus. For instance, when asked what an Aussie company would do if it was found to have run afoul of environmental laws, 66% said the company would abide by the rules either voluntarily or obey a court order.

No. 7: Austria

Austria scores highest on both fundamental rights and its criminal justice system. Of the 12 questions asked about perceptions of crime and the justice system in Austria, respondents were more optimistic than their peers in Western Europe and North America. For instance, on a scale from 1 to 10, with 10 meaning a very serious problem, do Austrians perceive systems designed to protect witnesses and whistle-blowers are deficient? Austria scored 1.4 on that one, when the average in the region is more like 4.4.

No. 6: New Zealand

The Kiwis do better than their Down Under neighbors, especially on matters related to the federal government. When asked if they could request to have access to information held by a government agency, how likely would the agency grant it, assuming the information is both public and properly requested- -100% said likely or very likely, more than any nation in East Asia and the Pacific.

No.5: Netherlands

Now we head to the best of the best. And it's all northern European. TheNetherlands scores highest on civil justice and regulatory enforcement. When asked to rank on a scale from 1 to 10 how serious was the problem of corrupt judges or a lack of court independence from the government's power, corruption was a zero and independence ranked 0.2, meaning respondents are very confident in their judicial system.

No. 4: Finland

Finland, judging by respondents there, has the best criminal justice system in the world. According to them, corruption of law enforcement and the courts is not a serious problem and the police have enough resources to catch the bad guys.

No. 3: Sweden

Sweden is No.3 overall, but No.1 in fundamental human rights. Eighty-five percent said they strongly agreed that religious minorities can freely and publicly observe their holy days and events on par with the average score in the region while another 86% said the media could freely express their opinion against those in power without fear of retribution, a higher percentage than the average regional response.

No. 2: Norway

Norway ranks No.2 globally, but is No.1 on matters related to open government, regulatory enforcement and civil justice. Respondents unanimously agreed that the government would provide public information if requested, and a little more than the regional average said their municipal governments were adequately doing their jobs.

No. 1: Denmark

Denmark ranks No.1 overall, but is also No.1 on issues related to constraints of government powers and absence of corruption. Seventy percent said that high-ranking government officers would be prosecuted and punished through fines, or in prison if involved in a corruption case.

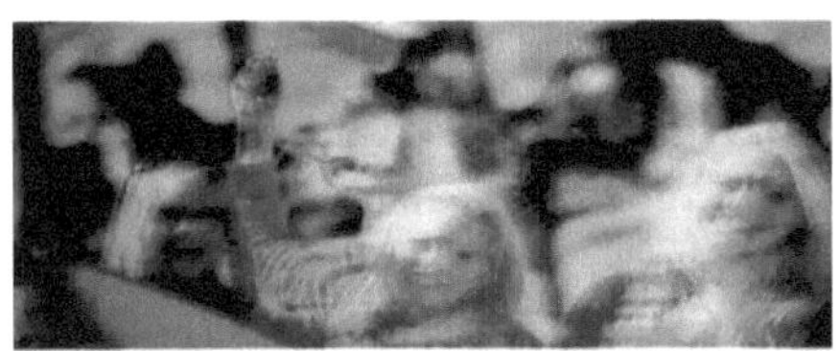

Cheering ladies

Some Reasons and Solutions

False Cases

Sometimes, people will make a mockery of the judicial system by filing of several false cases against their opponents to settle scores, thereby precious time of the court would be wasted in conducting the trial of those false cases. These types of frivolous and vexatious cases must have been nipped in the bud by imposing heaviest cost to get rid of the judicial backlogs to some extent.

Devoid of Merit PILs

Unmerited PILs are filed by persons either on behalf of themselves, their NGOs or throughAnyone else in High Courts and Supreme Court, which is a serious issue, as it takes up extremely important matters. But this exercise lags behind because of misconceived interventions by individuals that impede adjudication of important matters. All such endeavors have to be dealt with sternly to prevent such misuse of PILs and waste of precious judicial time. To stop it once and for all such NGOs' PILs be barred temporally as an interim deterrent measure or banned for life from filing non-meritorious PILs before any court in the country as rightly did the SC on Suraz India Trust, anNGO.

Timely Appointment of Judges

About 3.8 Cr cases were still pending in courts over the last decade. According to the sanctioned strength of Judges as of December 31, 2015, the Indian Judiciary was currently short of 20,502 Judges in lower courts, 1,065 High Court Judges and 31 Judges in the Supreme Court. If respective state governments or High Court would have done timely appointments of Judges, percentage of the pending cases could have been minimized drastically at least. Pending cases in SC has crossed 60,000.

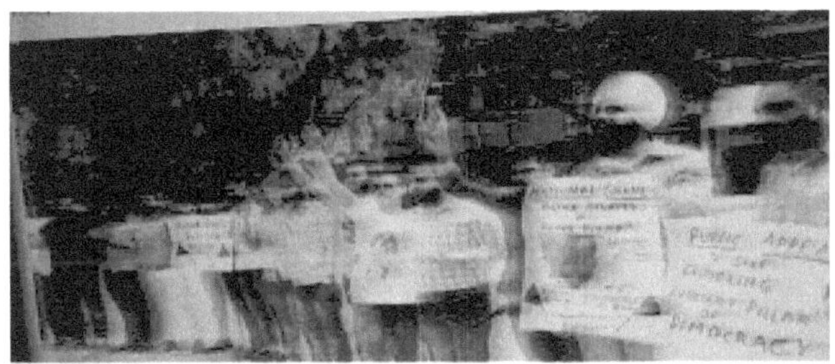

Protesting People

No. 66: India

Now heading towards the worst of the worst, peace and love India ranks poorly on order and security (95 out of 99) and civil justice (90/99).

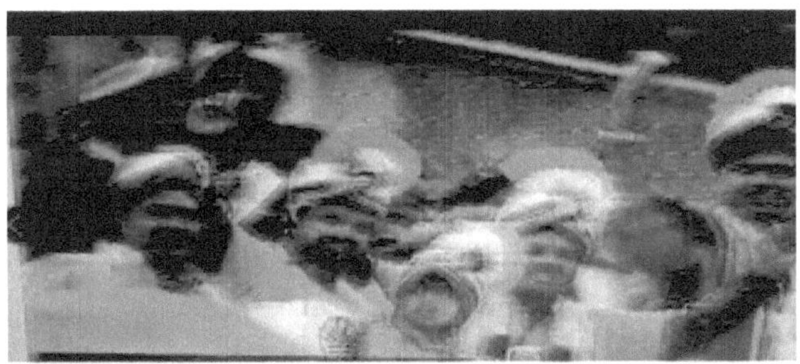

Celebrating People

Avoid Wrestling Bout of Judges

Our country's judicial system is based on Rule of law. Even Judges are curbed to take the law into their own hands. Judges flexing of their powers in terms of issuance of orders and counter orders to each other in the open courts on a futile contemptuous matter will certainly send a wrong message to the people, to whom courts are like temples wherein they worship justice. And above all Rule of Law means non-arbitrariness which can be ensured by guarantying freedom and one of such freedom is freedom of speech and expression. It is inherent in the Indian Constitution.

Rule of Law

There are two terminologies which are frequently used by the courts of law in India. Justice delayed is justice denied and justice hurried is justice buried. In the former case, it acts like a straw for a drowning man that applies to common litigants; but in the latter, justice is never delayed, but hurried, and therefore justice is buried that happens when the litigants, for example, are HC Judges, High Courts and Supreme Court.

CHAPTER THREE

Getting off my chest on the Demonetization:

Post-demonetization, we were witnessing human walls in the form of serpentine queues in front of each and every bank across the country, seemingly we were declaring our solidarity to the D. D (Demonetization Drive). The people who were badly affected by the said policy were the poor and the honest citizens of our country. They couldn't flee away as fugitives from the hard sell of the government's policy at once, but face it up whatsoever!

Queuing in front of a Bank

The honest citizens of our country had been destined to queue up before the banks by no fault of theirs; but for whose? The people waiting in the queues didn't owe anything to the banks. For example, ranging from 500(0) crores to 1000(0) crores, like some owed to banks in our country! I always felt like saluting the queued-up people as and when I come across them outside the banks. They were not willful defaulters; rather they had having sufficient money in their saving or current accounts. Notwithstanding leading an indebted life throughout their living time, that was more respectable life than an owed millionaire's (millionairess) or billionaire's (billionairess), majority of those innocent citizens had become economic refugees in their own country at least, even if it was for the time being. Could it be said that the vast majority of those indebted people were forced to queue up before the banks due to the default committed by some rich people to the banks in our country?

For whatever reasons, the economy drives of that demonetization had been introduced; its victims were ultimately the honest citizens of our nation. Be it for a day or over a month. Had it (demonetization) brought whatever positive results to our nation in the future, side of which, memory power of common man was going to be boosted by this demonetization strike? People could no longer live as idle in a cashless society, they might be alert and vigilant in such a society, in short, and demonetization had played the role of a memory booster in our country at the cost of tax payers' money in the name of digitalization.

The concept of cashless society was not a bad idea, like casteless or classless society! I personally supported the move, and was prepared to enjoy its fruits also; if it was genuinely intended to do. Demonetization was deemed to be a demon in initial days, as it caused so much of hardship to the common man; but situation had become better as time passed. So, countrymen(countrywomen), decided to let their all hardship and pain leave behind relating to the demonetization, as long-term gain might justify short term pain on the road to cashless country!!

On all the ongoing demonetization exercises, what I had felt the most interesting aspect was none other than the formal announcement about the demonetization by the P.M, who had played the demonetization cards close to his chest till last moment! Without any demur, that's it.

The government had succeeded in implementing the demonetization scheme in respect of its announcement of scrapping of old Rs.500 & 1000 notes by overnight, but failed in its execution by issuing new denomination (funny money) of Rs.2000 notes thereafter the demonetization.

People queue up in front of an ATM

Why that new Rs.2000 notes. I could not figure out any logic behind this idea! Honestly, if government was really concerned about the poor and the common man, why didn't it mint new Rs.1000 notes instead of relatively higher denomination of new (a chip off the old block) of Rs.2000 notes in that testing times. The time was not suitable for the introduction of new Rs.2000 notes, which made the situation more mesh. Besides that, the non-availability of new Rs.500 notes in liquidity in adequate quantities made the situation worst from worse. Otherwise, the Opposition would hardly get an opportunity to disrupt the parliament on demonetization issue while winter session was going on, that had made the demonetization hotter button.

CHAPTER FOUR

HIKE AGAINST HIKE

Motoring on motorbikes is always considered as a muscular activity, but safety and security are concerned riding is backspaced to backseat! People are preferred to be out on a day like this at least on two wheelers with a helmet. it is ironical that our motor mouth governments are interested in taking doctorates as how to monetize more from petrol and diesel in this pandemic situation than putting people's money where their mouth are.

Royal Enfield

The continuous increase sprees on petrol and diesel by the governments were making people combustible easily. It was quite natural, but what the governments were doing, it was oxidizing the people, who were already rusty through lack of incomes due to pandemic induced lockdown, and again making their lives even more miserable by that daily razzmatazz.

People who having motorized vehicles are in big dilemmas, whether to switch two wheelers from four wheelers and definitely vice versa will be going to burn a big hole in their pockets in those sporadic day to day episodes of price escalations on petrol and diesel, and now people are amid both pandemic Covid-19 and periodical price hikes on petrol and diesel.

Roofed three-wheeler

SWITCH OVER

A switchover from four wheelers to three wheelers or two wheelers or a shift from four-stroke gasoline combustion engine to electric vehicles (EVs) or compressed-air vehicles (CAV's) are the remedies to save one own skin in the future. Theory of operation of electric vehicles teaches us voltage (power to move) is generated from electrical energy into mechanical motion whereas a motor engine burn a fuel (petrol or diesel) to create heat which is then used to do work and likewise pneumatic motors use compressed air to move vehicles forward.

Two wheelers are aerodynamically moving fast without much drag from air, so, fuel efficiency is greater for two wheelers compared to four wheelers. Fuel efficiency is dependent on engine efficiency, transmission design and tire design. Oh, by the way, diesel engines generally achieve greater fuel efficiency than petrol (gasoline) engines. Even though, diesel rich in energy is not a solution let there be more diesel engine two wheelers in the market in the present form due to the emission norms couldn't be met, but two-wheeler makers are planning research to develop engines run on diesel. But we don't drag our feet to shift from four wheelers to two wheelers anticipating that the petrol and diesel trying times will come again.

Two-wheeler with canopy

RETRACT

More than 60% of the Indian population drives two-wheelers notwithstanding that the 82% of Indian do not own their own vehicles. In this backdrop, considering the present situation and feasibility two wheelers stand a chance to be enjoyed by the mass. Riding a two-wheeler in an open space is the most pleasurable part as well as profitable whereas the car will offer the constrained and enclosed environment, but who are going to see with their goggle-eyed your Jada Dubai and Passion Jewelers passion diamond shoes and Tadashi Shoji floral evening dress or Escada's Couture Swarovski crystal jeans in the moving car!

Canopied Three-wheeler

DETACH

Canopied two-wheelers cause less discomfort during rainstorms which shows the need for a fully-enclosed two-wheelers with a convertible roof which folds away when the sun shines and can be clipped back in place within a few seconds for when the rain comes and what if it has an electric powered roof operated by a single switch, and then it would be a good solution against the double whammy effects of both the pandemic covid-19 and the fuel price hikes!

TWO-STROKE

A two-cycle engine completes power cycle with two-strokes of the piston during only one crankshaft revolution is like a person's life with full of ups and downs of movements. In a two-stroke engine, the end of the combustion stroke and the beginning of the compression stroke happen simultaneously. In a two-stroke engine, the exhaust gases transfer less heat to the cooling system than a four-stroke, which means more energy to drive the piston and, if present, a turbocharger.

Child's Motor Vehicle

Compared to four-stroke engine, two-stroke engine have a greatly reduced number of moving parts. Production of two-stroke cars ended in the 1980s in the West, due to increasingly stringent regulation of air pollution.

FOUR-STROKE

The amount of power generated by a piston engine is related to its size (cylinder volume), whether it is a two-stroke engine or four-stroke design, volumetric efficiency, losses, air-to-fuel-ration, the calorific value of the fuel, oxygen content of the air and speed (RPM). A four-stroke engine is an internal combustion engine in which the piston completes four separate strokes while turning the crankshaft. A stroke refers to the full travel of the piston along the cylinder, in either direction. The four separate strokes are termed as induction, compression, ignition and finally emission.

Motorcyclist

If you and I decide that we will shed one pound of weight from our body, bring forth one minus child and own one less vehicle, then see, how much world is going to be benefited out of these sacrifices! But we are greedy and selfish people. The governments had increased fuel prices of petrol and diesel for the welfare of the poor recently. Demand for petrol and diesel was very meagre during the period of national lockdown in the country, wherefore, vehicle owners shall afford higher fuel prices since they are not starving. Every time governments had one or other justifiable reasons for fuel price increases. Earlier it was for building toilets for the poor! But, anyway, petrocurrency reaches the poor in one way or another, that's all it is. On the one hand one who does not want to have to one's name these kinds of two stroke or four stroke machines go for a hike, which physical activity on the other hand will keep ischemic and hemorrhagic types of strokes at bay.

CHAPTER FIVE

Hire a Typist, not an Advocate!

An advocate is deemed to have graduated in law from a law college or university in our country. He is not supposed to be a graduate in typewriting or shorthand! It is unwritten practice amongst the gentlemen senior advocates that they are committed in molding their junior advocates in their initial years to the professional life while inducting them to their office.

But such selfless senior advocates are very rare to meet the eyes nowadays! The majority of selfish senior advocates are belied that the right to practice law is the genus of which the typewriting and shorthand must be a specie! It is very disgusting. Should the junior advocates keep their mouth shut for such senior advocates?

Noticeboard

The ambition of a junior advocate to practice law is curtailed, if he or she joins a senior advocate office wherein a permanent typist does not exist. A junior advocate has a lot of acts to be performed towards discharge of his/her professional commitments than merely siting typing in the law office.

The right to practice law has been recognized and granted by Section 30 of the Advocates Act. A person who has obtained a degree of law is entitled to practice law just as any senior advocate. But senior advocates often thrust upon typewriting and shorthand on aspiring junior advocates without giving them proper guidance and advise on law practice.

This writer appraises and respects each and every job regardless of its impact and influence in the society without any underestimations whatsoever! But, having said that, hiring a junior advocate, without having scant regard to his or her aspiration to law practice is arbitrary and selfish and those senior advocates are mainly concerned with their own needs or wishes at the expense of consideration of junior advocates.

The junior advocates are in aid of their senior advocates in the Supreme Court, High Courts, Subordinate Courts, Tribunals or Other Authorities. The right to practice and the right to appear in courts are two different things, which all aspiring advocates wish to cherish in their minds.

If a junior advocate shall not be permitted to practice in court by a senior advocate, when a junior advocate wants to appear in a court. Which is solely determined by the Bar Council of India, and not by a mere senior advocate. Refusal by a senior advocate to permit a junior advocate to appear before court does amount to extinction of the advocate's legal entity as an advocate.

The advocates are to be the only recognized class of persons entitled to practice law. Every advocate whose name is entered in the state roll shall be entitled the right to practice throughout the territories to which the Advocates Act, 1961 extends. Advocates alone entitled to practice, no person shall, on or after the appointed day, be entitled to practice in any court or before any authority or person unless he or she enrolled as an advocate under the said Act.

The advocates are persons who are supposed to be the guardian of rule of law, as they have to advise the public at large in regard to the legal rights and obligations, maintenance of law and order and rule of law. The public view the advocates as men of knowledge, integrity and persons upholding the rule of law. The society had always viewed the profession of advocacy (not typography) as eminent and dignified. But unfortunately, some senior advocates do ignore it.

It is true that the rule framed by the Bar Council of India does not make out any distinction in dress or prescribe the design of a different gown or coat for a senior advocate, yet the distinction has been maintained and followed by a practice of long-standing, even prior to the Advocates Act of 1961.

The distinction between the senior advocates and advocates is that provides for right of pre-audience for senior advocates among others. The senior advocates constitute a different class within the advocates. Based on the ability, knowledge, experience, expertise and standing at the bar, an advocate is designated as a senior advocate. It is an honor and distinction conferred by the court in recognition of the ability and standing of the concerned advocate.

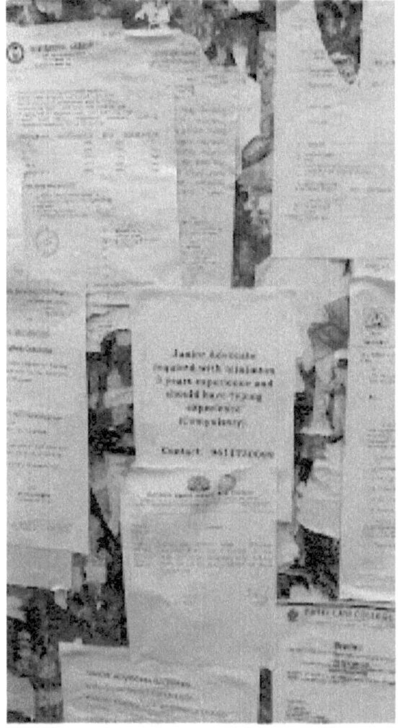

Notice Bored

Debarring junior advocates from appearing before court is unconstitutional being violative of Article 14 and 19(g) of the Constitution of India. I would be failing in my duty if I do not mention about one decision of the Supermen Court in Satish Kumar Sharma v. Bar Council of H.P., [(2001)2 SCC 365]: (AIR 2001 SC 509), the Supreme Court had occasion to make the following observations:

"The profession of law is called a noble profession. It does not remain noble merely by calling it as such, unless there is a continued, corresponding and expected performance of a noble profession. Its nobility has to be preserved, protected and promoted. An institution cannot survive on its name or on its past glory alone. The glory and greatness of an institution depends on its continued and meaningful performance with grace and dignity. The profession of law being noble and an honorable one, it has to continue its meaningful, useful and purposeful performance inspired by and keeping in view the high and rich traditions consistent with its grace, dignity, utility and prestige. Hence the provisions of the Act and the Rules made there under inter alia aimed to achieve the same ought to be given effect to in their true letter and spirit to maintain clean and efficient Bar in the country to serve the cause of justice which again is a noble one."

CHAPTER SIX

Hit people for Six:

This ATM was remained non-functional for quite a long time before the demonetization. Demonetization was supposed to affect those who are black marketers and currency fakers, but it literally hits the poor for six irrespective of both male and female and young and old.

Is it one's cup of tea?

This ATM is situated at City Civil Court Complex, Bengaluru, which now functions as a boon to several lawyers in this testing time by providing Rs.2000 notes, though it being an unbroken coconut now, on daily basis, so that lawyers like me need not roam around for seeking money in the city.

It is one of the ATMs in this area, which dispenses Rs.2000 notes to its users. This ATM is doing a great service to the lawyers as well as general public who come from all walks of life here. I am looking for Rs.500 & 1000 notes that the ATM is going to dispense in the coming days!!

Secular Castes and Secular Tribes:

(1) The President [may with respect to any State] [or Union Territory], and where it is a State, after consultation with the Governor thereof, by public notification, specify the castes, races or tribes or parts of or groups within castes, races or tribes which shall for the purposes of this Constitution be deemed to be Scheduled Castes in relation to that State [or Union Territory, as the case may be].

(2) Parliament may by law include in or exclude from the list of Scheduled Castes specified in a notification issued under clause (1) any caste, race or tribe or part of or group within any caste, race or tribe, but save as aforesaid a notification issued under the said clause shall not be varied by any subsequent notification. [Acc.Art.341 of the Constitution of India, 1950]

(1) The President [may with respect to any State] [or Union Territory], and where it is a State, after consultation with the Governor thereof, by public notification, specify the tribes or tribal communities or parts of or groups within tribes or tribal communities which shall for the purposes of this Constitution be deemed to be Scheduled

Tribes in relation to that State [or Union Territory, as the case may be].

(2) Parliament may by law include in or exclude from the list of Scheduled Tribes specified in a notification issued under clause (1) any tribe or tribal community or part of or group within any tribe or tribal community, but save as aforesaid a notification issued under the said clause shall not be varied by any subsequent notification. [Acc.Art.342 of the Constitution of India, 1950]

Schedule castes distribution map in India by state and union territory according to 2011 Census. Punjab had the highest % of its population as SC (~32%), while India's island territories and two northeastern states had 0%.

Schedule Tribes distribution map in India by state and union territory according to 2011 Census. Mizoram and Lakshadweep had the highest % of its population as ST (~95%), while Punjab and Haryana had 0%.

The Scheduled Castes (SCs) and Scheduled Tribes (STs) are official designations given to various groups of historically disadvantaged people. The terms are recognized in the Constitution of India and the various groups are designated in one or other of the categories. During the period of British rule in the Indian subcontinent, they were known as the Depressed Classes. In modern literature, the Scheduled Castes are sometimes referred to as Dalits.

But, in the present Indian scenarios, the terms secular castes and secular tribes shall be the appropriate and justifiable designations for the Scheduled Castes (SCs) and Scheduled Tribes (STs).

In 1935 the British passed the Government of India Act 1935, designed to give Indian provinces greater self-rule and set up a national federal structure. The reservation of seats for the Depressed Classes was incorporated into the act, which came into force in 1937. The Act introduced the term "Scheduled Castes", defining the group as "such castes, races or tribes or parts of groups within castes, races or tribes, which appear to His Majesty in Council to correspond to the classes of persons formerly known as the 'Depressed Classes', as His Majesty in Council may prefer". This discretionary definition was clarified in The Government of India (Scheduled Castes) Order, 1936, which contained a list (or Schedule) of castes throughout the British-administered provinces.

Word for word

The abbreviations of SCs and STs have nothing to do with one's own original caste name or surname but, in part XVI of the Indian constitution, regarding special provisions relating to certain classes, which contained two lists (or Schedules) these two lists of SCs and STs are included under article 341 and 342 respectively and officially the terms Scheduled castes and Scheduled tribes were coined. No one was born as SC or ST and moreover, it is neither a caste name nor a surname and much less than a family name. In brief, therefore, there are only two classes of people in India, those who are Scheduled castes and Scheduled tribes and those who are non–scheduled castes and non-scheduled tribes!!

The Scheduled Castes and Scheduled Tribes comprise about 16.6 percent and 8.6 percent, respectively, of India's population (according to the 2011 census). The Constitution (Scheduled Castes) Order, 1950 lists 1,108 castes across 29 states in its First Schedule, and the Constitution (Scheduled Tribes) Order, 1950 lists 744 tribes across 22 states in its First Schedule.

Thus, it is not a bad idea about appeasement of these classes of people by political parties prior to any general elections in anywhere in India. Is it so? Food politics and bed politics are two examples of wooing their support.

The reason behind all these *polytrics* is for nothing but eyeing to tilt the unfixed vote bank holding by these classes of people all over India. Schedule Castes (SCs) and Schedule Tribes (STs) form a little over 25% of the nation's population. Therefore, these classes of people can influence election results across the country. So, it is high time to form a political party in the name and style of the all-India secular castes and secular tribes federation or confederation to bring all the floating voters under one umbrella to contest elections by alliance with other political parties.

Since independence, the Scheduled Castes and Scheduled Tribes were given Reservation status, guaranteeing political representation. The Constitution lays down the general principles of affirmative action. The significance of the political party is the need of the hour at this juncture to field candidates outside reserved constituencies to win the elections thereby breaking the decades' old following taboos.

Cricketer

But, what about their social security. What are the steps taken by government to improve the situation of STs and STs?A number of laws were enacted to implement the provisions in the Constitution. One of the examples of such laws is <u>Scheduled Caste and Scheduled Tribe (Prevention of Atrocities) Act, 1989</u>. But, by the SC's March 20, 2018 judgment, the said act has become toothless and in effect, STs and STs have been deprived of their legal rights too?!

CHAPTER SEVEN

Losers Final

FIFA was founded on 21 May 1904, having headquarters at Zurich in Switzerland. FIFA is responsible for the organization of football's major international tournaments, notably the World Cup which commenced in 1930 and the Women's World Cup which commenced in 1991.

Zurich

Its membership now comprises 211 national associations. Member countries must each also be members of one of the six regional confederations in to which the World is divided: Africa, Europe, North & Central America and the Caribbean, Oceania, and South America. In number of teams 204(qualifiers) 32 (finals), current champions France (2nd title) and most successful team(s) Brazil 5 (times) The Fédération Internationale de Football Association (FIFA /ˈfiːfə/ FEEF-ə; French for "International Federation of Association Football") is an organization which describes itself as an international governing body of association football, futsal, and beach soccer. The tournament has taken place every four years, except in 1942 and 1946, when the competition was cancelleddue to World War11.

The tournament has been decided by a one-off match on every occasion except by a final round-robin (or all-play-all tournament, which is a competition in which each contestant meets all other contestants in turn) group contested by four teams (Uruguay, Brazil, Sweden, and Spain). Uruguay's 2-1 victory over Brazil was the decisive match (and one of the last two matches of the tournament) which put them ahead on points and ensured that they finished top of the group as world champions. Therefore, this match is regarded by FIFA as the de facto final of the 1950 World Cup.

World Cup started with 13 teams and now it is played with 32 teams. In the 21 tournaments held in 1930, 1934, 1938, 1950, 1954, 1958, 1962, 1966, 1970, 1974, 1978, 1982,1986,1990,1994,1998,2002,2006,2010,2014   and 2018, 79 nations have appeared at least once. Of these, 13 have made it to the final match, and eight have won. With five titles, Brazil is the most successful World Cup team and also the only nation to have participated in every World Cup final tournament. Italy and Germany have four titles. Current champion France, along with past champions

Uruguay and Argentina, have two titles each, while England and Spain have one each. The team that wins the finals receive the FIFA World Cup Trophy, and their name is engraved on the bottom side of the trophy.

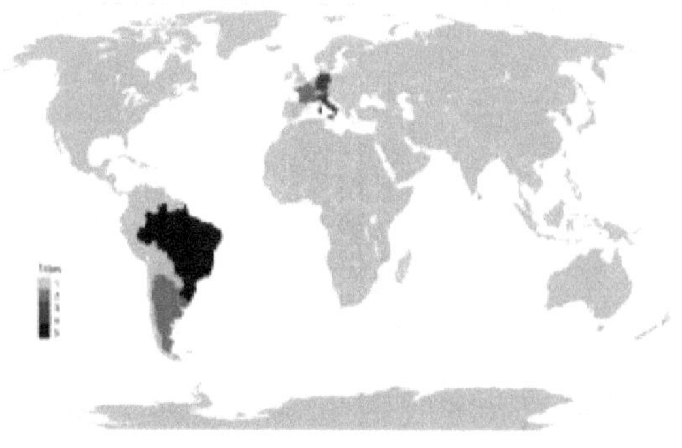

The globe

Unlike cricket, in football, team work is the path to success, and ultimately, the result would be a goal in the opposite side goal post. Team work that is what matters mainly in footballing. In cricket, on the other hand, one can perform well even in the absence of the team support, and it is an individual game in a team game.

Does size matter in the football? Yes, size matters. We can see there're some matches wherein strength overpowers skill quite often. In the foregone 2018 FIFA World Cup matches between Japan and Belgium and Argentina and France are some examples.

The 1930 FIFA World Cup was the inaugural FIFA World Cup, the world championship for men's national association football teams. It took place in Uruguay from 13 to 30 July 1930. FIFA football's international governing body selected Uruguay as host nation, as the country would be celebrating the centenary of its first constitution, and the Uruguay national football team has successfully retained their football title at the 1928 Summer Olympics. All matches were played in the Uruguayan capital, Montevideo, the majority at the Estadio Centenarion, which was built for the tournament.

Estadio Centenarion

The 13 teams were drawn into four groups, with Group 1 containing four teams, and the others containing only three. Each group played a round-robin format, with two points awarded for a win and one point for a draw. If two teams had tied on points to win a group, a play-off would have been used to decide the group winner; however, this was not necessary. The four group winners progressed to the knockout semi-final stage. Extra time was available in the knockout matches if the two were level after ninety minutes, but itwasnotrequired.

Over the period of time, there were drastic changes in selection, points and places, etc. of the nearing century old FIFA World Cup. In the first world cup, there was no qualifying matches, teams were entered by direct invitation. Now, there are qualifying matches for selection of the finals. And, in respect of points are concerned, 2 points for a win, 1 for a draw, and 0 for a loss in the World Cup up to 1990, and the same have been changed 3 points for a win, 1 for a draw, and 0 for a loss since 1994.Always 1 point for a draw and0 for a loss.

Similarly, with regard to places, the now-traditional third place play-off was not established until 1934, so the format of the 1930 World Cup is unique in not distinguishing between the third and fourth placed teams. Every world cup has had a third play-off, apart from 1930 and 1950.

Olympic medal

On an individual level, it is one more match in which to secure the Golden Boot, likewise, it can be more beneficial, if Golden Ball, Golden Glove, Fair Play and even YPA are decided on the basis of this match. One of the main criticisms against it that loser final is an easy money-making match. And to overcome this criticism with others, what to be made in LOTG subscribed to by FIFA. To make it more advantageous and exciting, why can't Loser's Final match be made for deciding the 1ˢᵗ runners up in the FIFA World Cup Tournament from now onwards.

After all, it is also a final, losers final! Then, there must have a winner, yes, there is. It can't be the 1ˢᵗ Champions, because the next day will be the crowning day of the new world champions. So, at least, second place be given to the third-place play-off winner, why because, they win the game defeating the opponent, as in the finals, one team win defeating the other!?

To make the losers final meaningful, important and interesting, be it for determining the 1ˢᵗ runners up in the entire tournament. And, third place for final losing team and fourth place for losing losers final team be awarded respectively. As a matter of fact, loser's final finalist is entitled to own the title of the 1ˢᵗ runners up since the team was played one match less than the actual finalist. But, by playing the losers final, the former equalizes to the later in terms of the matches played out.

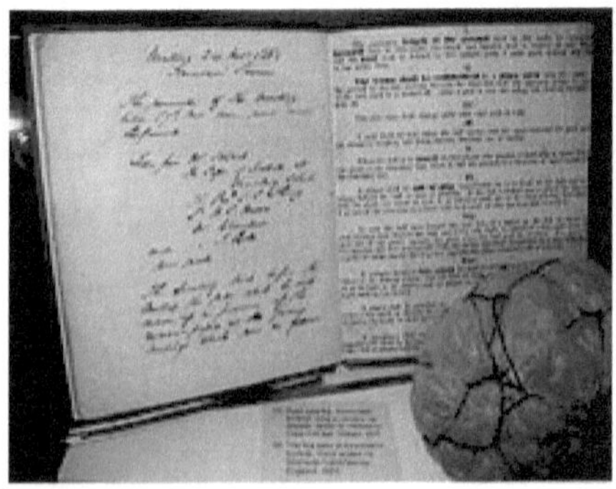

Bye-law

In this way, laws of the game were rewritten, in future, the words stupidity, pointless, chore, humiliation and waste of time, etc. can be avoided from the four corners of the world where billions of people watch this event in every four years of his or her life time.

The football

FIFA World Cup is such a huge event ever since it has taken place on this globe, so, it is not a bad idea to have two finals to determine the 1st Champions and 1st Runners-Up out of the tournament. Isn't it!?

CHAPTER EIGHT

MASK+SOAP=SHIELD

The cycle or bicycle was a bygone vehicle introduced in the19[th] century. It is a human-powered single-track vehicle, having two wheels attached to a frame, one behind the other for the purpose of movement like legs for a human being or an animal. A man is a rational animal unlike animal he or she tails them on its tail from time immemorial! What is the apparent difference between a human being and an animal? Simply guesstimate! Unlike tail, tie can be seen in Homo sapiens beneath a collar in the front.

Tied-man

It has been now more than my age figures in terms of number of days the national lockdown continues theoretically. The Covid-19 has tied down the world and his wife over right and thereby it has taken back all the comforts and luxuries out of the world and backed it off centuries ago gradually?!

People walking on railway tracks

The human's legs were on lay off after introduction of motor vehicles and more particularly after the invention of automatic transmission on vehicles like two, three or four wheelers. All and sundry have come back to square one or two now, i.e. on foot! A leg, a limb of an animal used especially for supporting the body and for walking?!

Cyclists

<u>CYCLAMENS</u>

Bicycle was the main means of transportation in those days and it is not a bad idea in readapting it for general fitness in this pandemic urged lockdown encouraged stay in period for mental as well as physical health to compact with corona virus. The bicycle's reintroduction will have an enormous effect in people, both in terms of recreation and of improving innate immunity in the absence of specific vaccination against the Covid-19 at presenttill posted on 30[th]May 2020. It would be better to allow the people to have peddling to commute on track rather than allowing the people to have pedestrianizing on footpath considering the benefits and risks involved in allowing it respectively. The most popular bicycle model and the most popular vehicle of any kind in the world is the Chinese Flying Pigeon! This valuable information is dedicated to the migrant workers whose exodus was a migraine for the governments a little bit, and moreover, please don't conclude that the cycle companies have created the corona virus?

Logo

HELMET PIGEON

A respirator is a mask worn over the mouth and nose to prevent poisonous gas, dust, etc. being breathed in, or to warm cold air before it is breathed. The point is here whether one should wear anti-pollution protection face mask & respiratory with carbon filter or a helmet with disinfectant in handy. It may be wise in one-time investment for a helmet rather than a mask or respiratory because helmet has two-in one use and it will protect one's head as well as respiratory tract while stepping out during this pandemic period. Police can't charge for not wearing a helmet indeed or a mask either, and please don't think that the helmet companies have recreated the corona virus?

Helmet pigeon

Please don't say that the disinfectant companies have brought the corona virus either! The Covid-19 is a communicable disease by droplet only for the hell of it. So, we can trust air we breathe and so as water we drink. But, the fact of the matter is that distrust, person to person or nation to nation. There is a general air of distrust in the atmosphere suspecting each other amidst this global pandemic going around the world. The Covid-19 is a very virulent virus but with masking and with soaping one can manage him or her touchily and at the same time injecting disinfectant as treatment was not as sarcastic statement but may be, a clean admission of ignorance.

Disinfectants

Usually most of the people wear helmet in their hands while riding two wheelers like scooter or bike etc. if there are no police checking on the way, similarly, and mask is supposed to be worn over the mouth and nose, but if there is no proper surveillance, people tend to push the masks under chin to rest on their necks! We should certainly discourage these practices of wearing helmet in hands or masks on the necks. But sometimes it reminisces while hearing and seeing news of stone pelting on health workers or police that some people are still living in the prehistoric period of the Stone Age!

Biker wearing helmet in hand

GNI vs. GDP

India is in fifth position in terms of GDP is concerned in the world economy and third when GDP is compared in terms of purchasing power parity (PPP). A more accurate indicator of a country's economic output is its gross income. GDP may be the standard method for calculating the size of a particular country or region's economy, but it does not account for all of the wealth generated by that nation. India is containing of the poorest of poor and the richest of rich states. Chhattisgarh is one of the poorest states in India about 1/3 of Chhattisgarh's population lives below the poverty line. 93% of people are poor in the Chhattisgarh state. Maharashtra is the richest state in India with GDP of 25.35 lakhs Crore. The economic capital of India Mumbai is the capital of Maharashtra with highest number of Covid-19 patients now is a surprise!

Caricature

DEBT DEADLOCK

The national debt of India amounted to around 1.8 trillion U.S. dollars in 2018.National debt, also called government debt or public debt, and is money owned by the federal government. It can be divided into internal debt, which is owned to lenders in the country and external debt, which is owned to foreign lenders. India's national debt today makes up almost 70 percent of its GDP. India's GDP is currently estimated at around USD 2.8 trillion. So, it is understandable that to achieve the target of 5 trillion-dollar economy from the fiscal year 2020 to 2024 by the government. Then only India can include in the group of countries of free of external debt. By the time let India become a private government. Until then every newborn in the country will be dependent of hundreds of thousands of rupees of debt!

In someone's debt

<u>LOCKDOWN 4.0</u>

Some people take Covid-19 as an opportunity and accordingly plan for future. The Covid-19 is not an opportunity for others who see it as a realization. World has broadly divided into two, the opportunists and the realizers. Nature is home for not only humans, but animals and plants, etc. Nature is first and after only world comes. The Covid-19 pandemic preceding national lockdown is as big as world lockdown, but much less than a universal lockdown! The nature can't be locked down a zeptosecond and it has no shutdown either. This is a checkmate. For those who are considering that the Covid-19 is an opportunity and for those who are visualizing that the Covid-19 is a realization respectively, and where are you now?

Locks

CHAPTER NINE

Promise is Promise

This was a true-life experience which not to be sneezed at its face value, because people are coughed up several lakhs and crores of rupees these days for owning own cars all over the world and including in India as well! So, it was regarding the Tata Nano car, a 624 cc 12 SOHC MPI Petrol engine with 15 liters of fuel tank capacity, therefore had got its momentum.

Front view of Nano

There was apprehension initially in bringing home the bacon, but finally after two years successful weightage, the thinnest and tinhorn had become part of life from the year 2010 onwards.

It was a wrong notion to take this no frills auto for a long drive on high way roads, but later realized that it was not an impossible task. It could be used for inter-city as well as intra-state travels with ease. It was manufactured and marketed by Indian automaker Tata Motors from Tata Group, which was founding ancestor of the Air India, with a launch price of one lakh rupees or 2,500 USD in the year 2008.

But, on road price or invoice value of the banger was one lakh plus and little less than one lakh, i.e.,1.9 bucks. It was unveiled at the 2008 Delhi auto show with an initial price of close to Rs.1 lakh, which was the ex-factory price, for the basic model despite cost escalations saying a promise is a promise! Anyway, wait was worth and it was the proud moment of owning wheels in such a time and for such a small price.

Rear view of Nano

Money is not everything, if money can procure all means of happiness, but money is not happiness itself! It doesn't buy life. Everyone has the ability to dream but not everyone has the willingness to truly chase their dreams. When people aren't living their dreams, they often have limited belief system. Dream chasing is for those who dare to take a chance to believe, that their dream is something more, than a thought or possibility. Even a standard version car is better than none to chase your enemy. If you could chase your big dreams with a little elf, which gives you power of driving thrill and then nothing could drive you away from that driving force.

It was a total dream come true years back for the very first time covered a distance of more than 500 kilometers at a stretch in this limo from one state to another state. It was really on top of the world feeling and just like conquered the world by a rear-engine hatchback coupe, the world's most inexpensive car then.

Right side view of Nano

The thrilling part of the driving experience was that a compact city car like the Tata Nano crate could be made a remote village car! The roads aren't made according to each and every car tire's compatibility on the roads. Similarly, all cars are not made each and every village, town and city roads keeping in mind. Anyhow, it was possible to rev up at 105 km/h on expressways and for national highways at 100 km/h with passenger capacity of four, 2 front + 2 rears.

The Tata Motors said bye–bye to the people's car in the year 2018. But it has been with us every time ever since from the date of its purchase. In letter and spirit, it was a city car hundred percentage as claimed by its manufacturer. A two-cylinder gasoline engine with a single balancer shaft jalopy was amorphous though. During the last decade, there were no single occasions for anyone of the hoop tie's tires was replaced and it was little over 30.k as per its odometer now. And, moreover, on spending on petrol this heap was really worth value for money.

Left side view of Nano

This motor was street smart enough and its drivability in city and more especially tier-1 city was astonishing. It could be passable on every nook and cranny of a city and turning, reversing, halting or parking wouldn't be a headache anymore. It was the best for drive-in and drive-through in the crowed places for those who are interested in cineaste and dine-out.

Tata Motors intention was to appeal to current riders of motorcycles and scooters in that point in time, but the fact of the matter was that the Nano was never really taken off by the public. Even though, riders who were wishing a roof top over their head while driving on roads in rainy or sunny days on their two wheelers, it could be a solution to their misery. It was like a small big umbrella, which had permanent showerproof and sun proof of canopy. In this present scenario of social distancing, its usage is felt more formidable since it reduces exposure to coronavirus and other germs. Its first aid box is more suitable to keep face mask and hand soap, which is neither a disinfectant nor a sanitizer as per doctors. Soapy water is considered best practice for protection against the Covid-19, because soap and water kill novel coronavirus by dissolving the virus's protective outer membrane, i.e., lipid coat.

There was an era of small car in the history of automobiles; hence one can't derogate small from big due to the former less fuel-capacity that is beneficial for the country and for the world as a whole too. In the post-corona era, a gear change is expected by some leading automakers from first-time buyers to smaller cars for personal commute some distance between one's home and place of work on a regular basis. Health experts confirm that the novel coronavirus is here to stay, so, to coexist with corona; a Nano car like automobile is a necessity for coveralls and if it is minimal enough for families to trade in their two wheelers and then it will play a new role in the new normal world ahead.

Man posing near Nano

It was still too expensive compared to a motorcycle, although it was identified as the most affordable car, a second-hand car that was more expensive when it was new gave more social status; the Nano was considered a "poor man's" vehicle, turning some people away. The failure had lain in offering it for peanuts, but you see the world through its Saint-Gobain glass is exactly same as that of super luxury cars show to you.

CHAPTER TEN

QUARANTINE IN THE TIME OF CORONA

In black and white, the lockdown was world-weary due to its closeness in India on a par with world–wide. True? A small virus has made the world completely upside down within no time. The humankind is armless before the tiniest, which forced them shut-in not able to go to no-go-areas.

People wearing masks

What a colorless world would it be a hundred years ago at the time of the 1918 flu, which was the cousin germane of the present one Covid-19, and the former was pet named as Spanish flu, a deadly influenza pandemic, which had infected 500 million people all over the world and the death toll was estimated anywhere from 17 million to 50 million or more, making it one of the deadliest pandemics in human history!

Sculpture

<u>SAD</u>

Seasonal affective disorder (SAD) has nothing to do with the Covid-19, but forced stay in period of one month or more than one month may start symptoms of sad such as mood off and depression, and signs and symptoms of sad may include having problems with sleeping, i.e., encephalitis lethargica, feeling sluggish or agitated and feeling hopeless, worthless or guilty. And above all the human behavior changes in response to the outbreak.

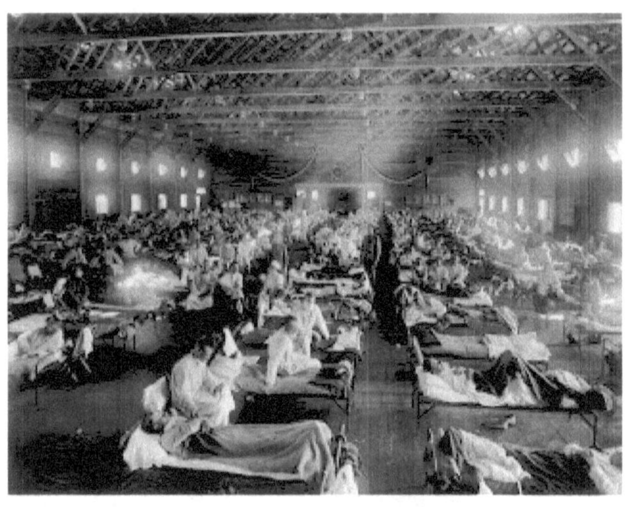

Patients in a general ward

A century has brought on sea changes to India as well as to the world ever since the fourth wave of 1918 influenza pandemic occurred in spring 1920. The pandemic in hand touch-and-go are vast in terms of wfh, (work from home) webinar, to name a few. Even the extended lockdown period may make one a loco, especially Gen X and Millennial, though google or you tube may alleviate problem to certain extent. For Gen-Z, there is play store in case of shops are required to be closed as a result of lockdown@ shutdown!

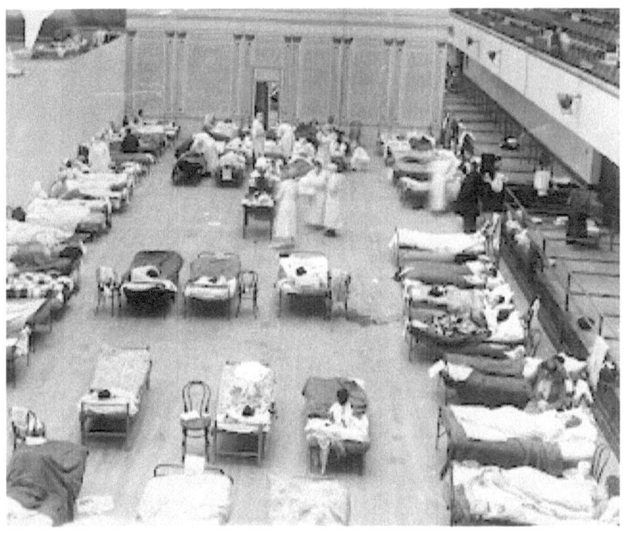

Patients on hospital beds

PHAR

In pharmaceutical industry particularly, now the second largest share of pharmaceutical and biotech workforce contributor in the world is India, where there was little or no access to aspirin, or acetylsalicylic acid (ASA) at the time of the unusual virulence of the 1918-1920 influenza pandemic, even there was anecdotal evidence of salicylate (aspirin) use in India. Indian drugs are exported to more than 200 countries in the world, with the USA as the key market, where to hydroxychloroquine (HCQ) is also exported recently, it is also being studied as a treatment for coronavirus disease 2019(COVID-19), like aspirin given shortly after a heart attack decreases the risk of death.

People boarding bus wearing masks

<u>TVL</u>

A large factor in the widespread occurrence of the 1918 flu was increased travel due to modern transportation systems made it easier to spread the disease in those days. In this ultra-modern era of transportations, it seems that the governments have taken a leaf out of that 1918 influenza, and therefore transport facilities were not arranged to the stranded migrant workers who were made walkathon along with children and pregnant women to reach their respective native places under the scorching sun in this Covid-19 pandemic lockdown stay in period.

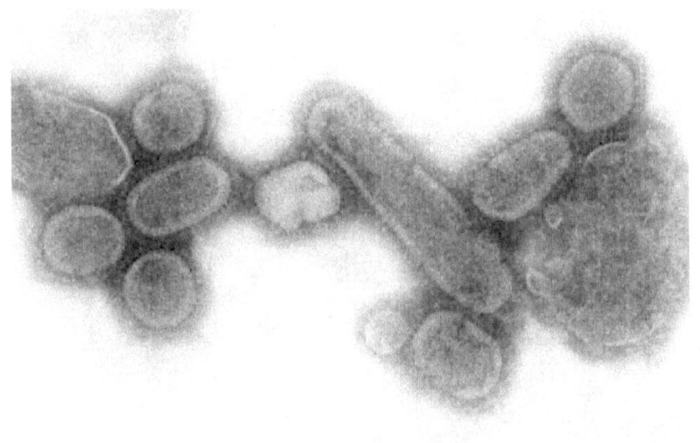

Microscopic images of virus

<u>VC</u>

While the development of video conferencing started in the late 19th century, i.e., before the 1918 flu (influenza) pandemic, the technology only became available to the public starting in the 1930s after the end of the pandemic, the video conferencing system technology's usage is greatly urged now and it has become the need of the hour in this Covid-19 influenced lockdown prompted social distancing times for telemedicine, distance education, etc. It is very difficult to maintain social distancing protocols always due to touch screen mobile phones!

Girls standing wearing masks

QUAR

There were places succeeded in preventing even a single death from the 1918 influenza through effective quarantines! With regard to global economic effects, many businesses in the entertainment and service industries suffered losses in revenue, but the health care industry reported profit gains. That is what is going to happen this time around. India implemented early and extensive non-medical measures like quarantine, etc. So that no additional adverse economic effects due to implementing those measures India suffered. "Quarantine" may be going to be adjudged as the "WOTY" (word(s) of the year) of the world, at least for the Indians in the coming days ahead!

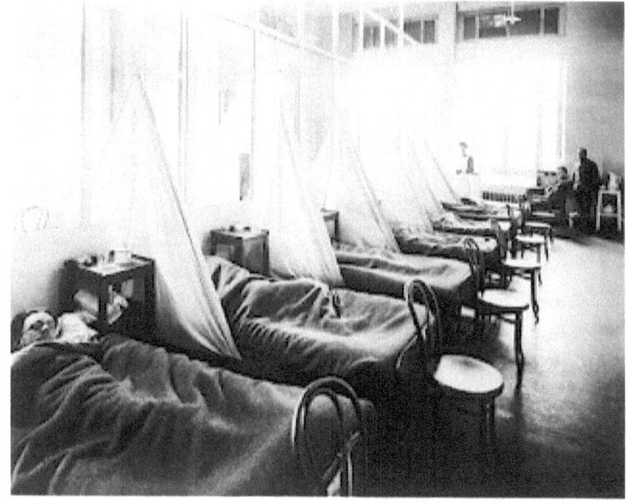

Army men on military hospital beds

GADGETRY

In the past, radio waves brought news and information regarding pandemic, but technology has been developing from time to time and audio signal has given way to video signal now, listening to viewing. Television (video) signal has a greater data rate than an audio (radio) signal. Lockdown have put huge dent on wallet of many, which does not offer an easy life in the new world, but cellphones, televisions, and Wi-Fi give some easiness, though they are not an easy street!

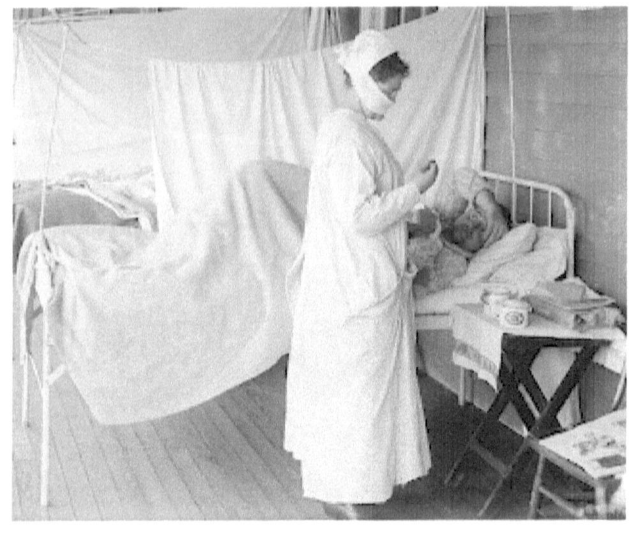

Nurse attending a patient

MASK

Earlier masks were unwanted items, unlike contraceptives, across all the medical shops in the country and abroad. Now masks and gloves are like protective shields out of harm's way! The theory of origin and emergence of the Covid-19 pandemic, whether originated, created or reconstructed, is subject matter of cytologists, but point is how to protect oneself from this pandemic by practicing non-pharmaceutical measures of social distancing and quarantine till medicine is readily available to everybody. Social distancing is already there among the haves and the haves not, so it is not a big issue in terms of keeping, following and continuing it among families, societies, or even counties! It is compulsory to wear masks now, but some are adamantly distancing from it thinking as very unprecedented!

Men in force wearing masks

Masks are various kinds, for e.g., toile masks, Halloween masks, oxygen masks and surgical masks, etc. In this corona induced lockdown period, it can't be masked that the demand for death masks have been decreased tremendously all over the world!

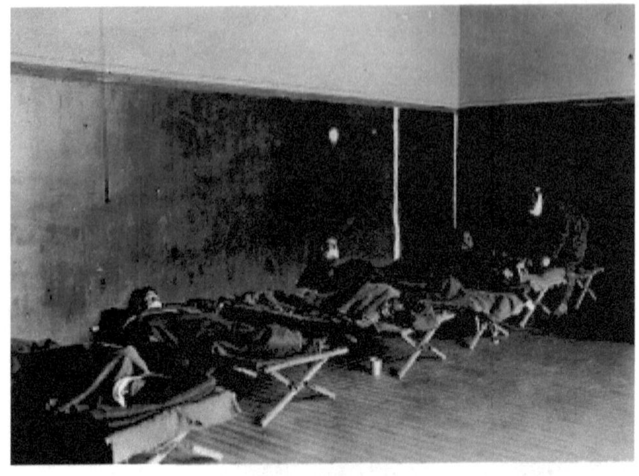

Doctor attending patients wearing PPE kit

LOCKDOWN 3.0

The blockage of leg work is due to either by the curb or by the fear of the microscopic new gen. Gen X and Millennial are the worst hit than Gen-Z by the lockdown @ shutdown not by one way but many ways. Lower income leads to malnourishment and poor hygiene. The comfort and consolation are social media platforms, online games, digital games, video games, etc., in this piss off time. With a smart phone in hand, one can vroom around geo-center in this lockdown period. But, once the lockdown is upheaved, life would be bouncy again in terms of movements of motorists and raising shutters of shops. Till then we can enjoy va-va-voom of panda car!

CHAPTER ELEVEN

Ten Micro Blogs

INSTANT JOKES:

"A man arrested for possession of heroine." [heroin]. It is one of the classic examples in misspelling of English words we see in our day-to-day life. When spelling is misspelled, it becomes meaningless. That gives instant joke. "By tickets to avoid penalty" [buy] is another example. We are not Englishmen to talk like them, but when we write something in English language, it must be correctly spelt, otherwise it will be ridiculed by others. The argument may raise against this that we also misspell our mother tongue sometimes. The fact is that if we misspell English or any of our mother tongue in such a way for that matter, it makes fun of its readers.

Laughing man

UNAPPEALING REALITY SHOWS:

It is the need of the hour to have in-house appellate authority in each and every TV Channels which conduct reality shows randomly that always becomes non-appealable from decisions of its panel of judge/s, wherein a contestant is not able to make an appeal from the decisions of any panel of judge/s. Where any party is aggrieved by a preliminary decision of a panel of judge/s should be entitled to make an appeal from such decision disputing its correctness in appeal. An appeal may lie from each and every decision and final decision. No appeal shall lie from a decision passed by the panel with the consent of parties. Where an appeal is heard by a panel of two or more judges, the appeal shall be decided in accordance with opinion of such judge or of the majority (if any) of such judges. Where there is no such majority which concurs in a judgement varying or reversing the decision appealed from such decision shall be confirmed. An appellate authority shall have power to determine a decision finally and to remand a decision to preliminary panel for its reappraisal. Then only partiality or intolerance of panel of judge/s on the basis of his/her personal choices may be curbed to a certain extent.

Whether really real?

EXIT IS THE STAR:

In any WhatsApp group, decency and decorum must be the touchstone to remove any participant or discard his or her post whatsoever it may be. If anybody being removed or any post of its participant being discarded without his or her consent will be only showing nothing but Group Admin audacious behavior towards its Participants. *Audi alteram partem* may be the motto before removing or discarding any participant or his/her post. Otherwise, real star will be the four-letter word 'Exit' in snubbing the Group Admin or Admins who may be one in number or more. Anybody can create WhatsApp Group in which there may be star-crossed to affluent one. Similarly, Admin may be person having high esteemed knowledge to much less than a lay person.

Arrow mark

CASTE BASED CENSUS:

Caste based census is not a good idea in terms of modern era of governance is concerned. The birdbrain exercise will only backfire the country to centuries ago instead of forwarding the nation to coming centuries with concept of casteless and classless societies. Even adding surname or caste name to the children's name by parents be blamed in the light of bitter experiences brought about this social menace to the Indian society.

It was a trend not to add surname or caste name after the first name of the children in the bygone generation. But surname or caste name is being thrust on children by the parents of the present generation who are injecting venom of communalism or casteism into the children knowingly or unknowingly by adding surname or caste name along with their children's name.

Representation

A NAME IS ENOUGH:

There can be seen certain loopholes in every branch of Indian laws that enables someone to escape from the crux of punishment. It will get off thousands of accused scot-free and consequent to that the innocent may be convicted or devastated. How to maintain equality before law or the equal protection of the laws in a country wherein people are divided unequal on the basis of class, caste and creed, etc. There are the haves and the have nots, the backward and the forward and religion and sect, etc. One has got by birth religion, caste and sub-caste, etc. apart from a name. Are these all required for a person to survive in a socialist, democratic and republic nation? Inequality before law or the unequal protection of the laws are everywhere.

Shakespeare

RACISM:

A 29-year-old MNC employee has been accused of rape and sexual exploitation by a 24-year-old woman whom he reportedly befriended through social media. The woman has filed a complaint with the police saying the man has raped her more than once and he allegedly refused to marry her saying that his parents would not approve of her as his wife as she was dark-skinned.

This is a clear case of racism. Racism is a universal phenomenon.it is practiced all over the world irrespective of class, caste and creed, etc. It is a social menace which comes out of human psyche. It is a feeling rather than of choice. Comparing to which, casteism is nothing but skin-deep and can be overcome by cashes. But racism is not like skin-deep but deep-rooted than that. In this context, if anyone calls Mr. Trump a skinhead, how can we say that it is false?

White supremacy or white supremacism is a racist ideology based upon the belief that white people are superior in many ways to people of other races and that therefore white people should be dominant over other races. Each and every people both at a collective and an individual level enjoy a structural advantage or privilege over other less white people than them or him. Apartheid, untouchability, black supremacy, white supremacy and slavery are reflections of racism in one form or other.

Stand in the schoolhouse door

WINE V/s BEER PARLORS:

The Abkari Policy framed by the State of Kerala from 1992 onwards with the object of gradually reducing the sale and distribution of liquor in the State. In 1992 with the intention of reducing the number of bar hotels, Government decided to restrict grant of FL-3 Licenses to only hotels having two stars and above. By 1996 Abkari policy the Government decided to ban sale of Arrack with effect from 01/04/1996.In 2002 as per the Abkari policy of 2002, an amendment was brought in the Rule restricting grant of FL-3 License to only hotels having 3 star and above classification. In continuation of the policy of the Government to reduce sale and distribution of liquor, Abkari policy of 2011 was announced inter alia restricting issue of FL-3 License to only having 4 stars and above classification.

Now licenses being issued to such 418 bar hotels, (61 per cent of the total bar hotels in the state) for sale and distribution of wine and beer in their wine and beer parlors (erstwhile bar hotels). So, the people, irrespective of their sex, man and woman may use and consume it in the pretext of medicinal purposes and government can be functioned at the cost its people health.

Three cheers!

COMPLETE BAIL OUT:

The accused was produced before the court and the court turned down accused plea for bail and sent him to 14 days police custody. The court witnessed high voltage drama powered by arguments and counter arguments between prosecution and defense against bail and for bail to the accused. It started with the question of accused custodial interrogation. The accused counsel who submitted that the case should not be considered for custodial interrogation for two reasons: There were no specific charges against the accused in the ongoing case and medical ground.

Accused suffers from hypertension, diabetes and chest pain, etc. and needed constant supervision of a doctor of his choice. Request for home cooked food was made from accused counsel based on his health conditions. Accused also sought a direction from court to avoid him from media lenses. Accused counsel also sought proper facility for him to sleep, including a proper bed outside prison cell, preferably in his own house!!?

Justice

DESIGN:

A designer is a person who designs. Design is a profession. The different types of design are costume design, fashion design and textile design, etc. The irony is that all are related to dress or clothes especially of women. As far as the designing and making of clothes to the ladies are concerned by the leading fashion houses, whether the dresses are complied with decency and morale of a person's sense of dress code.

As long as the haute couturiers are men, can one expect that craftsmanship and high quality from them who are high dressmakers by leading fashion houses in the world of fashion of dresses.

Clothing is collective term for garments. The wearing of clothing is restricted to human beings. Some clothing can be gender-specific. Physically dressing serves many purposes. Wearing clothes is also a social norm, as being deprived of clothing in front of others may be embarrassing, or not wearing decent clothes in public to the extent that genitals, breasts or buttocks are visible could be seen as indecent exposure.

Girl in modern dress

SCREEN TEST:

"I had not met a happy married man in my life". Said a Bollywood actress recently in a chit-chat weekly column published in a Sunday newspaper. Ms. clothes horse may not yet get an occasion to meet a happy married man who is not from the glamour field. There are indeed happy married men outside the film industry. The said actress has not come across any of them. Then the above opinion cannot be taken as a generalized one based on a specific case or cases.

What about married women in the same field. Are they happy or not? Considering the growing rate of divorce and strained relationships happening in the said field, it may be safely inferred that it is one of the sections of the society wherein institution of marriages is not successful and long lasting. People are totally unhappy and unsatisfied there.

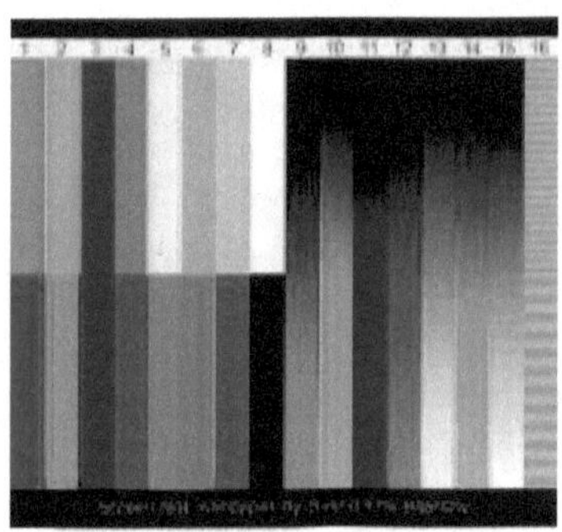

Different shades

CHAPTER TWELVE

The United States of India!

We, the people of India, having solemnly resolved to constitute India into a Sovereign, Socialist, Secular, Democratic and Republic and to secure to all its citizens:

JUSTICE, social, economic and political;

LIBERTY of thought, expression, belief, faith and worship;

EQUALITY of status and opportunity;

and to promote among them all

FRATERNITY assuring the dignity of the individual and the unity and integrity of the Nation.

Rightful protest

The unity and integrity were the soul criteria by which India, as a Union of States, decided by uniting several States on such terms and conditions into the Union, and formed a new State by separation of territory from any State or by uniting two or more States or parts of States or by uniting any territory to a part of any State; diminish the area of any State; alter the boundaries of any State and alter the name of any State. In a nutshell, the United States of India, that is Bharat, is a country consisting of 28 states 8 union territories. There are over a quarter of a million local government bodies at city, town, block, district and village levels in the above mentioned the United States of India.

India had proved its unity in many diverse situations in the past so as to say a few are wars, natural calamities, etc. Again, time has come for India to showcase its unity in diversity to the world how to manage a disaster like covid-19 pandemic when some of the developed countries have miserably failed to contain the spread of it exponentially! How? Before that something about WHO!?

The World Health Organization (WHO) initially shillyshallied about the Covid-19 and later only declared it as a global pandemic on 11th March 2020, exactly two months after 1st Covid-19 death reported in China on 11th January 2020, by the time the spread of the pandemic has flown more than hundred countries. Why was so much of dilly dallying in announcing, may be because the distinction between the words "pandemic," "epidemic" "endemic" and "outbreak" is regularly confused, even by medical experts!?

PM

The Indian citizens have wholeheartedly observed the "Janata Curfew"-the "Public Curfew"- called on by the PM on 19th March 2020 - a dusk-to-dawn curfew people to remain indoors on 22nd March 2020 between 7 AM and 9 PM. A few knew about that it was a precursor to the three weeks nation-wide-lockdown w.e.f. 25th March 2020.

The country's nation-wide-lockdown has constitutional validity so as to invoke relevant section and sub-sections of the Disaster Management Act,2005, a central act, coupled with entry 29 of the Concurrent List enumerated in the Seventh Schedule of the Constitution.

Being a developing country India has to have time to strategize its plans to cope with the new medical crisis occurred due to the Covid-19, and India was actually buying time by the 21 days lockdown for equipment by all means to save healthcare systems all over India.

The Bhore Committee Report, 1946, has been a landmark report for India, from which the current health policy and systems have evolved. The recommendation for three-tiered health-care system to provide preventive and curative health care in rural and urban areas placing health workers on government payrolls and limiting the need for private practitioners became the principles on which the current public health-care systems were founded.

India has a mixed health-care system, inclusive of public and private health-care service providers. The public health-care infrastructure in rural areas has been developed as a three-tier system like Sub-centers, Primary health centers and Community health centers. On the basis of the distributional pyramid, currently there are 722 district hospitals, 4,833 CHCs, 24,049 PHCs and 1,48,366 SCs in the country as on 7th December 2016.

The public health and sanitation, including hospitals, primary health centers and dispensaries as well as conservancy and solid waste management including police are being the States subjects, despite the declaration of the lockdown by the Union government, its implementation lies with the States. So, the first step of the Union government after the announcement of the one-day Public

Curfew was to meet all the stakeholders of the government machinery, especially the PM was close-knit with all the CMs (the "Chief Ministers" of the States) frequently apart from lakhs of Village Panchayat presidents from across the country, the opposition parties' leaders, sporting stars, etc. through video conferences.

<u>LOCK-DOWN 2.0</u>

As expected from all quarters, the PM on 14th March 2020 announced extension of the national lockdown until 3rd May 2020 with the strong messages that people stay home and stay safe, and thereby immunizing oneself naturally to infection by eating and resting well?!

Campaign

While the whole world was going on auto pilot mode of WFH for a quite sometimes due to the Covid-19 lock-down, there were scenes seen in city like Berlin and many parts of the USA including the USI (The Union States of India) against coronavirus related lockdowns. In every democratic country, there must have opposite parties.

Opposition is the strength of the democracy. Protesters in Pacific Beach called Covid-19 "a lie" and people who were not following social distancing orders or wearing facial coverings when gathered to protest. Slogans like "Fear is the Real Virus", "My virus my choice", "live free or die" and "stay-at-home orders to slavery" were come out with the gatherers.

Cop

In the German capital, Berlin, the demonstrators wore T-shirts accusing the government of "banning life" while others called for "freedom". The far-right Alternative for Germany (AfD) party accused the government of exaggerating the risk posed by the virus and had called for the immediate reopening of all businesses.

Slogan in corona time

SLOWDOWN

The outcome of lockdown is slowdown. This is a situation in which financial emergency has arisen. The framers of the Indian constitution have made provisions in the constitution for the government to tide over situation like this vide Article 360, which is herein below extracted briefly with your permission.

PROVISIONS AS TO FINANCIAL EMERGENCY

According to clause (1) of the Article 360 of the Constitution of India, 1950, if the President is satisfied that a situation has arisen whereby the financial stability or credit of India or any part of the territory thereof is threatened, he may by a Proclamation make a declaration to that effect.

PROVIDED that if any such Proclamation is issued at a time when the House of the People has been dissolved or the dissolution of the House of the People takes place during the period of two months referred to in sub-clause(c), and if a resolution approving the Proclamation has been passed by the Council of States, but no resolution with respect to such Proclamation has been passed by the House of the People before the expiration of that period, the Proclamation shall cease to operate at the expiration of thirty days from the date on which the House of the People first sits after its reconstitution, unless before the expiration of the said period of thirty days a resolution approving the Proclamation has been also passed by the house of the People.

And, as per clause (3) of the said Article, During the period any such Proclamation as is mentioned in clause (1) is in operation, the executive authority of the Union shall extend to the giving of directions to any State to observe such canons of financial propriety as may be specified in the directions, and to the giving of such other directions as the President may deem necessary and adequate for the purpose.

As well as, vide clause (4) sub-clause (i) of sub-clause (a) says that, notwithstanding anything in this Constitution any such direction may include a provision requiring the reduction of salaries and allowances of all or any class of persons serving in connection with the affairs of a State.

Finally, sub-clause (b) of clause (4) of the Article 360 says that, it shall be competent for the President during the period any Proclamation issued under this article is in operation to issue directions for the reduction of salaries and allowances of all or any class of persons serving in connection with the affairs of the Union including the Judges of the Supreme Court and the High Courts.

Mass burial

FEED-RATION

The Indian government has saved hundreds and thousands of people's lives by declaring a blanket country-wide lockdown in time in the wake of the Covid-19 global pandemic, a Vis Major. India could triumph so far, for my money, not by money power, rather than India's unity to federate. It's a structural triumph. *Unus pro omnibus, omnes pro uno* (One for all, all for one) is a Latin phrase, which is squarely applied to India's triumph. Please look at the preamble of the constitution, which emphasizes to promote fraternity. This is the time showing compassion for your fellow citizen who is in crisis and thereby assuring the dignity of the individual and the Union government feeling pity for the States governments thereby promoting the unity and integrity of the nation.

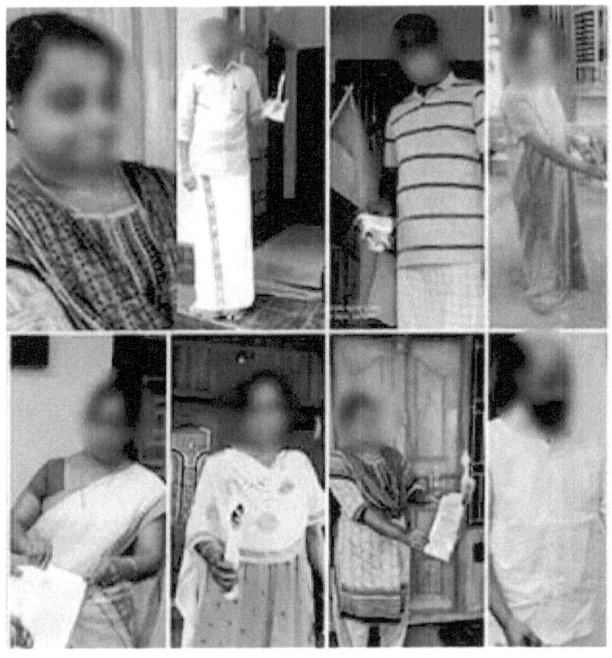

Burning protest

TRIUMVIR

It is true that this stay in period may have made a hole in the GDP of the country, which is till outdistancing of Covid-19, but the lives saved by the purported lockdown can't be measured in terms of money. For that generation to come would be grateful to India for preserving future generation from Covid-19. This is not the time to maintain the social distancing protocol of the Covid-19 by the three organs of the government, i.e., legislature, executive and judiciary. If a government, State or Union, goes for funds raising measures for Covid-19 relief in terms of reduction of salaries and allowances of all or any class of persons in connection with the affairs of a State or Union, the judiciary mayn't forejudge those initiative in its orders citing technicalities. This is for a common cause. Freeze, defer or cut, in whatever way it is called, the government borrows some resources for time being from its employees to lend it to the poor who are not salaried class, but coolies. The government employees who are not lost their salaries, unlike the poor self-employed but rather gained their salaries (immunities) in this stay indoor period during the lockdown due to Covid-19 pandemic. So, be sportive, take it as a plasma therapywhich aims at using the immune power gained by recovered persons to treat sick persons.

www.ingramcontent.com/pod-product-compliance
Lightning Source LLC
Chambersburg PA
CBHW032022140726
47988CB00017BA/974